HOME THOUGHTS

James Kirkup

Red Squirrel Press

First published in the U.K. in 2011 by
Red Squirrel Press
Holy Jesus Hospital
City Road
Newcastle Upon Tyne
United Kingdom
NE12AS
www.redsquirrelpress.com

Red Squirrel Press is represented by Inpress Ltd.
www.inpressbooks.co.uk

ISBN: 978-1-906700-45-4

Printed by Martins the Printers,
Sea View Works,
Spittal,
Berwick-upon-Tweed,
TD15 1RS

Foreword

Those who have received a letter from James Kirkup (the South Shields born poet and author) will know the delight of discovering what else is included in the envelope: a postcard, a Japanese memento and, often, an especially written poem. Throughout the forty-five years of our friendship I usually responded by sending James local photographs or Gazette cuttings. At Christmas time I would send a calendar or a greetings card from the collection sold at the Central Library and, almost by return of post, I would receive a new poem inspired by the image. This collection is the culmination of these exchanges.

The book contains evocative images of South Tyneside both past and present together with related poems in which James recalls his childhood in the town. Before James Kirkup passed away in 2009, we had discussed the possibility of producing such a book. So I am especially grateful to Hildred Whale at South Tyneside Libraries and Sheila Wakefield of Red Squirrel Press for helping me to bring James' hopes to fruition.

Dorothy Fleet

Dorothy Fleet

October 2011

Archivist and Curator of the James Kirkup Collection

www.thejameskirkupcollection.co.uk

Acknowledgements

I would like to thank Dorothy Fleet, Hildred Whale, South Tyneside Libraries and the artists and photographers for their invaluable help and support, this book would not have been published without them.

The Old Town Hall, South Shields and *Cleadon Water Tower* are from original watercolours by Tom Finch. Tom Finch (1918 – 2003) was a multi-talented North East artist, renowned for his exceptional skills in watercolour, puppetry (marionettes), sculpture in most media including wood, bronze, metal, papier-mache, and for many years was a highly respected tutor and mentor to numerous amateur artists through his Tom Finch Art Group.

Jarrow Town Hall by Ken Hogg. Ken Hogg (1937-1997) was a graphic designer and well-known local artist. He studied design at South Shields School of Art and worked for Design Group (Newcastle upon Tyne) and Fenwicks (fashion illustrations). He also produced theatre foyer displays and designed programmes. Ken mounted several exhibitions in the North East and his watercolour paintings of local scenes have sold worldwide from the USA to Australia.

With acknowledgements to South Shields artist John Harvey for his winter time watercolour paintings of *South Shields Town Hall, The Old Library* and *Christ Church, Jarrow.* www.harveyart.co.uk
King Street and *St. Stephen's Church* are from original watercolours by Arnold Keedy. *The Ferry 'Tynemouth'* painting is by local South Shields artist Martin Woods. *South Shields Market* is by local artist Ron Thornton, well known for his beautiful book 'The River Tyne : From Sea to Source'.

The photographs, *The Lifeboat, The Swans, Whitburn* and the *Conversation Piece* are with kind permission of South Tyneside Council taken by David Whale, Keith Bardwell and Tony Cutter for South Tyneside Libraries; *The Groyne* and *Souter* are by the late John Moore who was chief photographer with The Shields Gazette and *Marsden Bay* and *Westoe Village* are by local photographer and film maker, Gary Wilkinson. www.northeasternfilms.co.uk

South Tyneside Council

Dedicated to the memory of James Kirkup,
with love and respect

THE KNOCKER-UP

All the mornings of my early childhood
began at five o'clock, when the knocker-up
tapped on the window with his pole -- a sound
that haunted my sleep and wakened me betimes
from nightmares of school sports, the horrors
of weekly visits to the municipal swimming baths --
then the terrors of mathematics, physics, chemistry
that poisoned every day with foul gases of theorems.

But my real education had already begun at home
at six o'clock in the morning (when
my father was "in work") and I helped my mother
to lay, build and light the kitchen grate
after raking out the remains of last night's cinders --
while my father shaved in the sink's icy water
in the freezing scullery on its dark backyard,
"having a scrape" under the gas mantle's precarious
hive of light shivering at every footfall from upstairs.

After a quick trip to the dark outdoor netty
I sat by the fire, watching it "take" and slowly
feeling its warmth on my hands and bare knees.
As my mother made the breakfast for my father,
I sat eating a slice of bread and dripping
and drank my mug of scalding tea. -- At last,
humping his tool bag, my father in all weathers
set out for the shipyards or the new estates --
steady carpenter who had wanted only
to follow his captain father in a life at sea.

Then I still had a couple of hours to spend at home
before running down the streets to the school bell
with its urgent note of suppressed bullying rage.
I still had two hours with my library books -- reading
the whole of Dickens (kids' stuff), Arnold Bennett,
Thomas Hardy, D.H. Lawrence, Wordsworth, Rupert Brooke -
all "too old for you" -- but I never felt it so.

Because I had been awakened early --
even on Sundays I was up at five o'clock
to start the week's new library books --
a solid engagement, habit never grown out of.
-- And eighty years later, I know I am still
obeying that tap on the window of life's knocker-up.

SOUTH SHIELDS TOWN HALL IN SNOW

It's ten minutes to five, a snowy day --
brief break in the clouds --
but more snow coming up
from the North Sea.
That model ship -- weathervane
perched high on top of the solid clock tower
still seems to be making heavy weather.

But the statue of Queen Victoria,
snow draping the dark folds of iron robes --
is the orb of Empire still in that hand? --
still stands imperturbably on her lone
pedestal, in a fir tree's noble shade.

Is that a glimpse, just behind her, of one
of those naked nymphs who used to surround
the Town Hall plaza, lifting electrical lamps --
but they, too, have long since been cleared away,
as too provocative in their nudity

for working lads whose fathers had taught them
the old Tyneside rhyme?-- "Of all the statues,
great and small, there's none like them outside
the Shields Town Hall"-- (Paris Opéra copies;
they had become a hazard for leering drivers).

There is a touch of sun, casting shadows
of passers by, and of a tall street lamp.
The stolid main building glows in brief warmth,
but no one has cleared the snow off its flight of steps,
leading to a cherry-red door that offends the stone.

-- But soon we shall hear the clock strike five
solemn strokes, the usual pigeons will flutter
briefly and settle again in the tall
openwork tower's curious cage -- that bell
haunted the long dreams of my mis-spent youth

across the road, in Fowler Street, and right
opposite that grave clock face, that seemed to
be pressing its moonful of sinister figures
against my bedroom window with mocking
defiance: "Time and tide wait for no man..."

But in spite of everything, I am still
keeping those patient guardians waiting --
their every quarter, every hour
is struck for me, however far I roam,
with grave tones that poisoned every day and night

as dream-shadows crept to the beaches down
the weirdly-named Ogle Terrace, that led
to dark parks, and maritime horizons
and the lonely pier of dreams I haunted
night after night, with time's distant warning buoys.

CROFTO
CROFTONS
LIPTON
ALLSOP
THE FAMOUS CLOTHING STORE
MERCERY SEAMENS'
A Keedy

SPELLBOUND

This picture must have been painted
from a turn-of-the-century photograph.
(Judging by the women's long dresses
and capaciously brimmed hats).
But it is mostly men who inhabit
this King Street snow scene -- still
as a snow scene in a crystal ball.

It is viewed perhaps from the steps
of the Old Town Hall in the Market Place.
The men stand in groups at the corner
of "The Famous Clothing Store" --
seamen's outfitters and general mercery
opposite the domed brick corner tower
of Crofton's with its oeil-de-beouf
ornamental windows under the dome,
high above the tall drooping lily of
a municipal street lamp and its slim shadow.

Though it has been snowing
the tram outside the shop is open-topped
with a single brave passenger –
or is it the ticket conductor up there
where the sensitive trolley is fishing
for nothing in the stilled air?

On all the rooftops, outcrops of red brick,
tall reefs of chimneys with multiple chimneypots
rising out of the snowy seas of frozen slate
and Lipton's proud ornamental gables –
it's fourteen chimneypots all in a row
(and none of them smoking).

The idle men are mostly in cloth caps
and wear no overcoats -- hands in pockets
as they stand around gossiping
and waiting for the pubs to open.
Only two men are wearing overcoats,
and they are apart from the out-of-work groups.
There are no children: in those days,
at this time of morning they were all in school.

In the far distance, another tram, double-decker,
is passing under the railway bridge for steam trains
that run to Tyne Dock, Jarrow, Felling,
Gateshead and Newcastle-upon-Tyne Central Station.
-- But this main shopping street is empty of traffic
except for a single cyclist riding between the tram tracks.

There are two soaring red flagpoles
without any flags or banners.
But Crofton's slanted outdoor window blinds
shield the suits, the hats and dresses
and the caverns of hanks of coloured wools
from what appears to be only a weak sun.

Somewhere on the right along this street
stands the Empire Music Hall,
The Golden Lion Hotel, and the Penny Bazaar
where my mother was a young lady assistant.

Two or three public clocks show blank faces –
Appropriately -- for here time has stopped
forever, except in the spellbound memory.

GHOSTS OF THE PAST

Drained almost of all
colour -- shadows on fresh snows
illuminating
this public square, where curving
tram tracks transport the viewer

to a still centre,
transfixed by a spell of ice.
-- Rows of iron posts,
their rigid guard plastered by
winds from the north that painted

long stripes down one side,
topped each with an egg of snow.
Winter's withered leaves
still cling to one little tree,
trunk bare in its metal corset.

Church of Saint Hilda –
a spectral presence whose clock
tells no time under
a low sky of breaking cloud.
-- On this almost empty square.

three tiny figures:
one is sheltering under
the classic arches

of the Old Town Hall -- modest
yet noble council room cube --

eighteenth century
windows of the Mayor's Parlour
with railed balcony --
those elegant flights of steps
meet on the central archway.

This bare market place
once crowded with busy stalls:
first taste of prawns,
the salted heat of fresh chips
(vinegared paper cornets).

Puritan whiteness
of the domed bell-tower on
the snow-slatted roof.
-- Good Fridays, first primroses
for marchers, led by brass bands --

Children greet Easter
with eggs, oranges, banners,
in full heart and voice
sing our Methodist hymns – Now
echoes in this barren square.

FREE LIBRARY
MAXIM ALE
JAHarvey '99

THE OLD LIBRARY, OCEAN ROAD, SOUTH SHIELDS

I still seem to hear the griping grind and groan
of the monumental double-decker trams to the Pier Head
outside the sober windows of the Newspaper Reading Room
with its smells of fresh newsprint and coal miners' old boots --
four year-old standing as if for hours with Uncle Martin
among the readers' armies of unemployed trouser legs
--Racing Results, Football Scores, Situations Vacant --
I was lost in forests of sloping racks far overhead
bearing "The Shields Gazette & Shipping Telegraph".

"Way above your little head" severe librarians at the issue desk
gravely informed me when I brought my books to be stamped
with expiry dates for Poe and Arnold Bennett as I showed
my first library card, hot in my eager hand -- I still
remember the fascinating squeak and metallic thud
of the hand-operated date stamp -- modern efficiency –
filling a fresh-labelled book with haphazard days and weeks
of Conrad, Wells, Woolf, Hardy, Shaw, Shakespeare, Shelley...
dark green tomes of music scores -- Wagner, Scarlatti, Verdi, Chopin...

The palatial tiled entrance hall contained a sailing ship,
accurate scale model enshrined in fingerprinted glass
forever grounded at the foot of a noble flight of polished stairs
conducting me to the Art Gallery's pastoral landscapes and wild marines
with a gorgeous view of the Scala across the street -- Mae West!
Chaplin, Garbo, Fred Astaire, Jack Buchanan, dear Jeanette MacDonald,
enormous technicolour heads above passing tramcar roofs;
then to the twilit, odorous museum, floor-polished jungle
of stuffed parakeets, cobras, tigers, wolves and walruses
their glass eyes glaring among fur and feathers, bevies of butterflies
from another world, another life that I dreamed of, and longed
to discover, in lands and oceans far from Ocean Road -- the Criterion,
embalmed in beer, the tailor's, pails and spades, and Notarianni's
ice-cream parlour rumoured to be a den of adolescent vice...
while outside the soaring ecclesiastical windows the upper decks
of earth-bound tramways sounding foot pedal warning bells
with chinking trolleys in magical showers of sparks, blue flashes
were my only dreamboats groaning and grinding round the bends

of gleaming, sand-filled tracks and points to the Market, Tyne Dock,
Laygate, The Fountain Inn, the Cut's wild echoings running
to Westoe Village, embowered in ancient trees -- on to Harton,
Caldwell and Cleadon Hills, the ghostly White Horse.
--I still go there in dreams -- along the mile long South Pier;
lose myself among Trow Rocks' haunted bays, clifftop Marsden's
sea-smelling grottoes, its green bathing-tents, the deck chairs
where the idle rich could mingle with the out-of-work
on sands that were a luxury free to all, the sea a paradise for ever.
Library closing time -- distant warnings from the Town Hall chimes.

R.W. THORNTON '90

THE OLD CLOTHES STALL, SOUTH SHIELDS MARKET

The old jackets rub shoulders
on the racks of life and death,
the crumpled trousers all undone
swing in a driving wind,
a boneless abandon,
soft-shoe shuffle in the sands of time.

These skeletons out of their cupboards
are human, still warm with dying.
There are crumbs in their pockets,
dust in their turnups,
broken feathers in best hats,
glad rags in the seats of their pants,
in elbows where the striped lining
pokes out like fractured bones.

Laid away, the painter's dungarees
are dingy white, stained with forgotten schemes
for houses decorated out of sight.
The cobbles spread their broken flag.
On wooden stalls, tented with clouds
of canvas, a grimy resurrection lies.

Here are the collier's clogs, the seaman's denims,
the housewife's shifts and Sunday coats.
-- These are the limbless ghosts
jumbled here on the old wooden stalls,
heaped in confusion or suspended
like out-of-work puppets in
the north wind of curious hands and faces

stirring them in their graves
like the bones in the churchyard of
St. Hilda's, on the resurrection morn.

THE LIFEBOAT IN THE SNOW
(at the Wouldhave Memorial)

From my too-distant childhood, I still remember
that elegant Victorian lantern tower and its clock --
the carved stone panels below the ornamental balustrade.

Today, that mysterious little door I could never open
is painted a fashionable cherry-red that offends the stone.
But the old-fashioned horse trough drinking fountain
is now gone -- no more horses -- not hygienic enough
for our modern times plagued by diseases then unknown.

But I remember the heavy iron cup on its clinking chain --
its musical note when some careless boy just dropped it
to swing against the wall below -- a jangling dangle.
Thirsty dogs or beach ponies came to drink there in summer.
"Don't you dare drink out of that cup!" my mother warned me.
"You never know what you might catch!" -- But I yearned
for forbidden joys that other children freely sought,
so when my mother wasn't looking -- or wasn't there --
I drank my fill from that heavy metal cup of secret
sorrows that never seemed to pass away from me.
-- I still remember the touch of the metal, and its taste
against my teeth as I sipped its divinely icy waters.

It stands there still -- memorial to William Wouldhave,
local and universal hero, inventor of the lifeboat, that saves
from shipwreck so many mariners in North Sea gales. -- She still
arrives in time to rescue me in Time's uncharted storms.

This is the stop where my tram-tracks sank into the sand
and the driver with a hastily-lighted Woodbine seized
his trolley rope and ran back behind the tram to set
the chinking runner on the wire in a Guy Fawkes display
of blue, green and golden sparks as I went dashing up the stairs
to get a front seat on the rocking double-decker boat of lights.
But there are now no more rocketing ricketty old trams.
In this photo, it is always Sunday morning, so still --
only that cherry-red doorway disturbs the peace.

And the Tyne Lifeboat still goes sailing on
through all the years, back to when I was a boy
through all the years sipping my forbidden elixir from my iron cup.
-- I can still hear the clattering of its iron chain
that still seeks to bind me to the northern past
as the world sails on through all my dreams of snow.

CHURCHYARD IN THE SNOW
(Saint Stephen's Church)

She founders -- not in waves, but in the snow --
this noble vessel with her sacred prow
hoisting its cross above the chasmed deep,
the tombs and trees of a marine graveyard.

Her vast roof like a tilted deck flings up
a spume of seagulls from the snow-slung tiles
unleashing shuddering avalanches
as waves, higher and higher, drop lower

and ever lower down these tombstone deeps
sunk in a winter's timely blossomings
with wreaths of snowflake petals, heavenly spray
whirling in ethereal north-easters.

But this great vessel does not founder, and
for a moment the storm is stilled...while two
ladies dressed in mourning of bygone days
stroll, sweeping the rutted snows with long skirts.

One shakes snow from her lowered umbrella:
the other walks with her, hands in her muff,
their Sunday-go-to-meeting bonnets firm
and sober on their hatpinned hair -- phantoms

from another age that still endures here
with their snow-stormed church of the first
Christian martyr, he who was arraigned
for blasphemy, and stoned to death... But his name

means "wreath" or "crown" -- Greek stephanos --
and endures like a lighthouse in the church
of my childhood, where I first learnt to read
books stormed by words, like churchyards in the snow.

THE GROYNE, SOUTH SHIELDS

That familiar beach with the sandshoed sand is now
smothered in fresh snow, still virgin, though also scuffed
by the feet of phantoms -- lone visitors now vanished.
The white snowballs of local seabirds are still afloat
in the gentle shallows, or fringe a brief hem of shingle.
Here and there, a hank of seaweed, black mermaid hair.

In the sun-struck distances, across the River Tyne, there lies
another snowy landscape of a moon less familiar – image
of some distant childhood memories – ferry landing voyages
to another northern town – but another world, another life.
-- For me, in boyhood -- and even now -- just to cross the Tyne
was to set foot upon the fantasy of some unknown foreign land...

But the strangest sight of all here is that small pier
sticking out its snowy tongue at Tynemouth "ower the watter",
as at the Viking torments of the North Sea north-easters
that brought us those ancestors long after the Romans came
to this broad estuary always with its arms wide open --
welcoming guests, or defying blonde-bearded invaders with

colossal storms, brute cliffs of breakers that obliterated
whole heavens, and the hells of shipwreck rocks -- And yet,
on that small spit of stone, almost at the defiant tip
of its salty tongue, a stocky quadruped, a doll's house dream,
this geometric red-painted two-storey lighthouse stands akimbo --
lost landing-craft from some other still undiscovered planet.

SOUTER LIGHTHOUSE IN THE SNOW

Snow has plastered all the landscape, and the skies still
threaten even heavier falls. But the present whitenesses
of this overnight avalanche are paled by all the brilliance,
immaculate, of the lighthouse walls, whose inner light
goes on shining when greater lamps are dimmed.

For a spirit, light itself, inhabits still by day
the tower's crimson-armoured head and gleaming walls, graced
by that broad band of scarlet on their perfect flanks
all glistening in a fleeting shaft of wintry sun --
inextinguishable radiance illumining this lantern's turning world.

SWANS IN THE PARK

Those ornamental wrought-iron benches
that graced childhoods in the South Marine Park --
arm-rests showing leafy squirrels eating nuts --
replaced now by chill green or red plastic
and what look like see-through litter bins.

All the romance of this park by the sea
was symbolized for me by those cast-iron
squirrels sporting in metal foliage.
-- The magic of the park has all been lost
for one who knew it in less humdrum days.

Even this heavy snowfall cannot hide
such Parks Committee ugliness, that makes
almost everything else look very cheap.
-- But they cannot take away the classic
dignity of these swans upon the lake.

The kind gardeners have broken the ice
to provide a little sanctuary
for the unflurried swans I loved to feed
with bits of bread and dripping from my snack;
mandarin duck flotillas bob there too.

None can ignore the immaculate grace
of these snowy-feathered birds – the beauty
of long necks, the heads' brooding orange beaks
that try to repair some invisible
imperfection in their feathery foam.

Beyond the ice, the winter shrubbery
tries in vain to hide the everyday
monotony of railings and the banal road.
-- Meanwhile, these gracious creatures welcome us
to their imperfect paradise of snow.

THE INSTALLATION
('Conversation Piece')

What appear at first sight to be nine or so bundles of rags
or amateur haystacks dumped on a floodlit open-air dance floor
are now seen to be humans -- long arms, tiny hands -- look, no legs! --
like outsize bowling-pins swathed and swamped in clumsy crinolines
turning dumb belles into dumbbells: not much conversation here!

And what sort of ballroom is this bare esplanade where grotesque
bottlegourd débutantes pin down their shadows in wait for the first
bars of a swooning Prokofiev valse on weeping and wallowing strings...
But where is the eager rush of passionate Imperial Guard cadets
to sweep these ladies away in brave white uniformed embrace?

These ladies are having a very long wait for suitable partners --
for the Student Prince or the dream escort clicking delirious heels
in formal invitation to an intoxicating waltz's well-known rubato
that groans with barely-suppressed lust for a flirt, a touch of sex
among the Chinese lanterns lending romance to pedestrian shrubbery...

But where are the soft rosy lights, the florid table decorations,
the powdered talc of a radiantly polished dance floor deck
tilting in oceans of scent as it aches to be danced on? -- Alas,
the grand gallop dreams these lovely love-lorn ladies share
are their own bleak shadows, on feet sunk in lakes of cement

under the glare of a battery of coldwar anti-aircraft searchlights
making them look even more lost and lonesome, forlorn in fog.
Their one changeless backdrop is sand, the grey stone blocks of a long
pier (distant swivelling lighthouse flash), a navigation lamp's red
metal dwarf under threatening skies billowing over this desolate void.

But still these well-bred young ladies in their bouffant ballgowns --
(or are they maternity wear?) stand with shaved pates, awaiting
armies of ardent suitors to ravish invisible limbs in high-heel pumps
into the seventh heavens of a rapturously yearning grande valse! But
they linger in vain as rising tides swamp their ironclad skirts

and carry them all dancing like castaway bottles without messages
into the dark North Sea, there to bob up and down like a fairground's
figures of fun or abandoned mooring buoys – lightless, plunging
and drifting away in the long hesitation waltzes partnered by death --
into the snowy fjord graves of ice in faraway Noroway afar, afar...

1902

TWO VIEWS OF JARROW

"Jarrow – the Holy City" as I used to overhear
certain sarcastic Geordies calling it with native wit
as we were passing through the place in train or bus.

But in their irony there was a deep affection,
as well as grim memories of those Jarrow Marchers
who tramped the length and breadth of Britain

to stir the consciences of regions better-off down south
with banners of unemployment and the doleful dole
hanging their black clouds upon our northern skies...

-- These two paintings show another view of history.
On both there is a truly noble redbrick Town Hall
(dated 1902) with its elegant octagonal dome.

The rich colour of that edifice warms the heart
after the snowfall in Ken Hogg's nostalgic scene
with its patient horse and cart by the old lamp post

and all the people in their outmoded winter clothes
-- the girls and women in long skirts, bonnets, muffs
the men in mufflers and felt hats, cloth caps standing

hands in pockets --and a boy in knickerbockers too --
It is a scene from Louisa May Alcott's immortal
"Little Women" -- with all that Victorian charm.

On the other side of the road, there stands
in John Harvey's painting, the superfine steeple
of Christ Church, opposite the earth-bound Town Hall --

the same place, but the scene now is modern
with cars, trucks, a yellow van -- and everyone
is in sober contemporary clothes and footwear

in this view still pasted by a recent snowfall
that has clothed overnight one naked churchyard tree
in pure white blossom -- and the snow's not stopped

for some are sheltering under their umbrellas.
-- Is that one tall smoking chimney at the vista's end?
A century divides these two visions of the everyday
with a sense of place -- the same but different.

WESTOE VILLAGE

These grassy banks are those I knew
some eighty years ago, in childhood
and in youth. And those white wooden rails
protecting the cobbled path in
its pleasant grove of tall trees
beyond which the tiled roofs of
gracious houses lifted their chimneys.

In the shadows of those trees
white balustrades slope down
to the broad road, to the lane
leading to Harton, along which
I learned to ride my bicycle,
or raced on borrowed roller skates,
between fields and mooing cattle.

-- But best of all I remember
that echoing narrow passage under
the village mansions, then the yard
behind the Fountain Inn, the noisy street
outside the hospital's tall brick walls --
and the moaning tram-cars grinding round
the bend to Westoe, their trolleys
jerking, jingling, shooting sparks --
and that ghostly sound of the first
corporation tram car in winter dark
moaning up the hill, and squealing round
the corner, past the little post-office
making for Tyne Dock or rural Caldwell
and the foreign hills of Cleadon.

In pyjamas under the kitchen gaslight
of 48 Ada Street, our house and home,
with my bread-and-dripping, cup of tea,
and my father, carpenter's toolbag
on the shoulder of his worn dungarees,
leaving for work in shipyards of the Tyne
as I read my latest library book
by the fire -- "Dombey and Son" or
Shakespeare plays, Chaucer, Jane Austen
by the fire in the grate...

Until the school bell
began to toll, and I rushed down
the backlanes to the safety of Osborne Terrace,
and the hell of Westoe Secondary School,
my favourite nightmare.

Tom Finch

CLEADON WATER TOWER

Italianate, in ornamental weathered brick,
this tower, hydraulic, this seamen's landmark,
lighthouse without a light on Cleadon Hills,
stands like some ancient classic apartment block
from Umbria, giving a touch of class and mystery
to our workaday, smoky Tyneside harbour town,
rivalling those other elevated local piles
the Town Hall clock tower, black as soot
and scarlet-banded clifftop Souter light-house.

But our grand Water Tower, a successful marriage
of hydrostatics and classic architecture, oversees
the slate roofs of colliery rows, the new estates
and the pit head's twinkling wheels of winding gears.

Tower that seemed to throb with unseen cataracts,
its mystery surrounded by a long stone wall
running round its demesne of rhododendron clumps --
our fairy palace gazed at longingly
through wrought iron gates, always locked.
-- When I was small, it seemed so enormous --
my first skyscraper in a rare summer sky, supervising
a picnic on the hills. My father flew a kite
while my mother knitted socks and poured the tea
from a battered thermos flask (its dented metal cup
too hot for me to hold, wrapped in her hankie).

We were sitting on a grassy slope
that I loved to roly-poly down.
But one day I rolled so fast I couldn't stop, and
landed in the big stand of stinging nettles
under the Tower's soot-blackened brick embattlement.
-- My face, hands and knees, extravagantly blistered,
stung worse than the panic blushes and my tears
as my parents collected handfuls of dock leaves
and rubbed them on my wounded limbs, my pale face
patched with angry red -- that old remedy seemed to me
a touch of magic from my mother's gentle hands,
so tender to my childhood torments, soothed by her kiss, her laughter.

I still did not realise how brave she was,
but I knew I could be sure of all her loving care,
that compensated for my father's silences.

Here now, in this picture of the Water Tower
it is winter -- but I am in a foreign land
where sun blazes from a permanently blue sky
upon the mountain ski slopes
where all is joy and laughter at slips and tumbles;
and I see the painting of this tower on the hills
at Cleadon -- in deep snow, under bare trees...

But there the gate still stands, dividing me
from that strange demesne of haunted childhood
behind the grey stone wall --

where there are now no more nettles.

WINTER IN WHITBURN

There they stand still -- those three park benches in
the white of Whitburn. I used to lean my bike against the back
of that one at the front of this old photograph
and sit there all morning writing those early verses –
my own kind of watercolour sketches, in words and worship.

I liked those sturdy ornamental end pieces
supporting the few worn planks of seat and back
copiously carved with arrowed hearts entwining
pairs of initials joined in a lover's ribbon knot --
that elegant ironwork -- both delicate and strong.

The decent old village lay all around its green
like a protective barrier against a world growing mad.
The square church tower roof's modest pyramid of slate
seemed oriental among the foliage of summer, autumn, spring.
House gardens then were open to the road, and full of flowers.

Today, no one is sitting on the snow-sheeted seats
and there are no footprints yet in the perfect snow
that lies there for all the village in its bare old trees.
-- But I can still see a shadow sitting on that bench,
in peace, alone as always, scribbling lost poems.

MARSDEN ROCK

There is a sinuous pathway all along those curving clifftops.
With the fields on one hand, the North Sea on the other,
how often I pedalled idly along its treacherous
humps and hollows! It required a steady touch on
the bouncing handlebars, while under the saddle
the leather toolbag's spanners rattled as I jounced along.

If it had been raining, my tyres imprinted on the clay
those interweaving daisychains whose simple flow diagrams
traced the problems of their undulating graphs.
--There was never any need for the hoarse warnings of
my rather rusty bell, whose squawkings mingled with the cries
of indignant gulls; for I always seemed to be the only one

with the mad impulse to map the great bay's perilous path.
But I always kept a keen eye on the cliff's grassy verge
where the wild flowers -- blossoming gorse, dandelions, clovers --
bloomed in a floral fringe above the grander borders down below
of North Sea rollers casting wide lassoos of wind-blown foam
with gentle thunderings upon the rocks and caves and sands.

In this photograph, how brightly those memories shine!
The whole bay seems to be basking in a summer sun
that must be low, because it throws cliff shadows
far out across the beaches and the waves -- but it's November
and under unseasonably clear skies we can see as far
as the mouth of the Tyne, the white thimble of our lighthouse.

--And just beyond the creeping shadows there stands the Rock
detached, long battered into shapeless shape by winter storms
that soon will rage again upon its crumbling bastion
where gannets and Arctic gulls would come to nest
and lay their eggs that no intruders' hands could ever reach...
its flat top wild and mossy still and pathless round the edge.

M Woods 2000

THE FERRY "TYNEMOUTH"

The River Tyne today looks choppy in a breeze off the sea
that rocks roughly a moored rowboat and twists the smoke of funnels
on a pilot craft, the cargo vessels at anchor and this old ferry
whose square hoisted gangplank shows it has just left
the ferry landing and its slanted bridge that leads to the Market.

The pilot's up in his cabin above the top deck under the funnel
where a few adventurous passengers are holding on to the rails
while the rest remain cosy in the cabin down the steps.
The whole contraption starts waltzing as it heaves and turns
to the throbbing music of the churning paddles.

And you can almost hear it hooting its three hoots
as it ploughs its way among the river traffic
saluting a three-masted sailing ship with rolled-up sails
and directing its elongated tub-shaped monstrosity towards
the mists and smoke of the Fish Quay in mysterious North Shields.